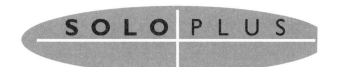

Flute

with piano accompaniment

An outstanding collection of classic Christmas tunes
expertly arranged for the beginning soloist with piano accompaniment
in printed *and* digitally recorded formats.

Amsco Publications
New York/London/Paris/Sydney/Copenhagen/Madrid

Cover photography by Randall Wallace
Arranged and performed by David Pearl

Order No. AM 967593
US International Standard Book Number: 0.8256.1819.3
UK International Standard Book Number: 0.7119.8515.4

Exclusive Distributors:
Music Sales Corporation
257 Park Avenue South, New York, NY 10010 USA
Music Sales Limited
8/9 Frith Street, London W1D 3JB England
Music Sales Pty. Limited
120 Rothschild Street, Rosebery, Sydney, NSW 2018, Australia

Printed in the United States of America by
Vicks Lithograph and Printing Corporation

Contents

Angels We Have Heard on High

Traditional French carol

Moderately fast (♩ = 120)

Deck the Hall

Traditional Welsh carol

The First Noel

Traditional English carol

It Came Upon a Midnight Clear

Richard Storrs Willis (1819–1900)

Go, Tell It on the Mountain

Traditional African-American spiritual

God Rest Ye Merry, Gentlemen

Traditional English carol

I Wonder as I Wander

John Jacob Niles (1892–1980)

Moderately slow (♪ = 116)

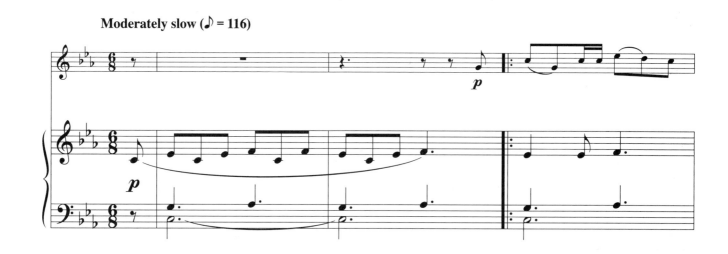

Jingle Bells

James S. Pierpont (1822–1893)

Lively (♩ = 92)

Flute

Cover photography by Randall Wallace
Arranged and performed by David Pearl

Order No. AM 967593
US International Standard Book Number: 0.8256.1819.3
UK International Standard Book Number: 0.7119.8515.4

Exclusive Distributors:
Music Sales Corporation
257 Park Avenue South, New York, NY 10010 USA
Music Sales Limited
8/9 Frith Street, London W1D 3JB England
Music Sales Pty. Limited
120 Rothschild Street, Rosebery, Sydney, NSW 2018, Australia

Printed in the United States of America by
Vicks Lithograph and Printing Corporation

Amsco Publications
New York/London/Paris/Sydney/Copenhagen/Madrid

Angels We Have Heard on High

Traditional French carol

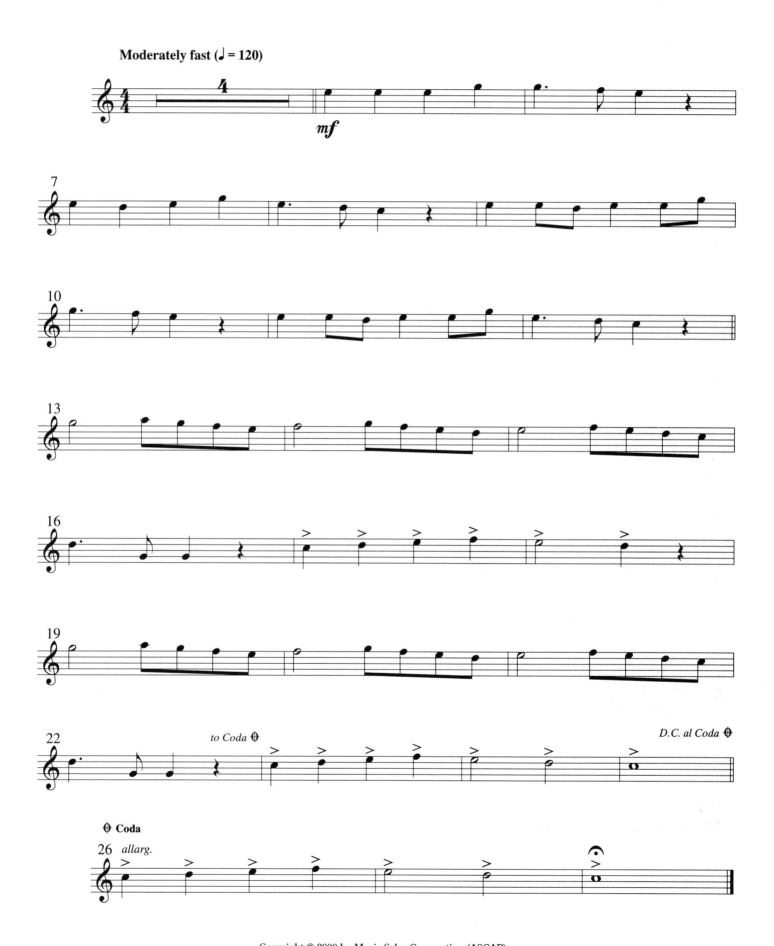

Deck the Hall

Traditional Welsh carol

3

The First Noel

Traditional English carol

Moderately (♩ = 88)

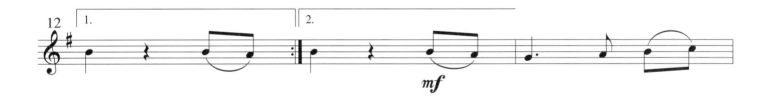

It Came Upon a Midnight Clear

Richard Storrs Willis (1819–1900)

Go, Tell It on the Mountain

Traditional African-American spiritual

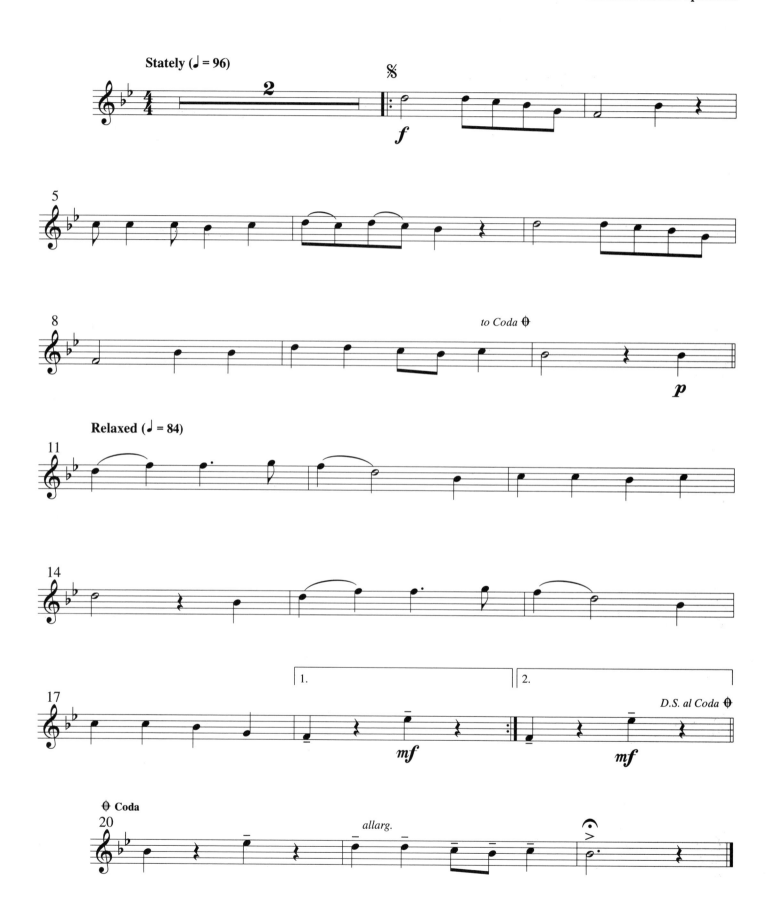

God Rest Ye Merry, Gentlemen

Traditional English carol

I Wonder as I Wander

John Jacob Niles (1892–1980)

Jingle Bells

James S. Pierpont (1822–1893)

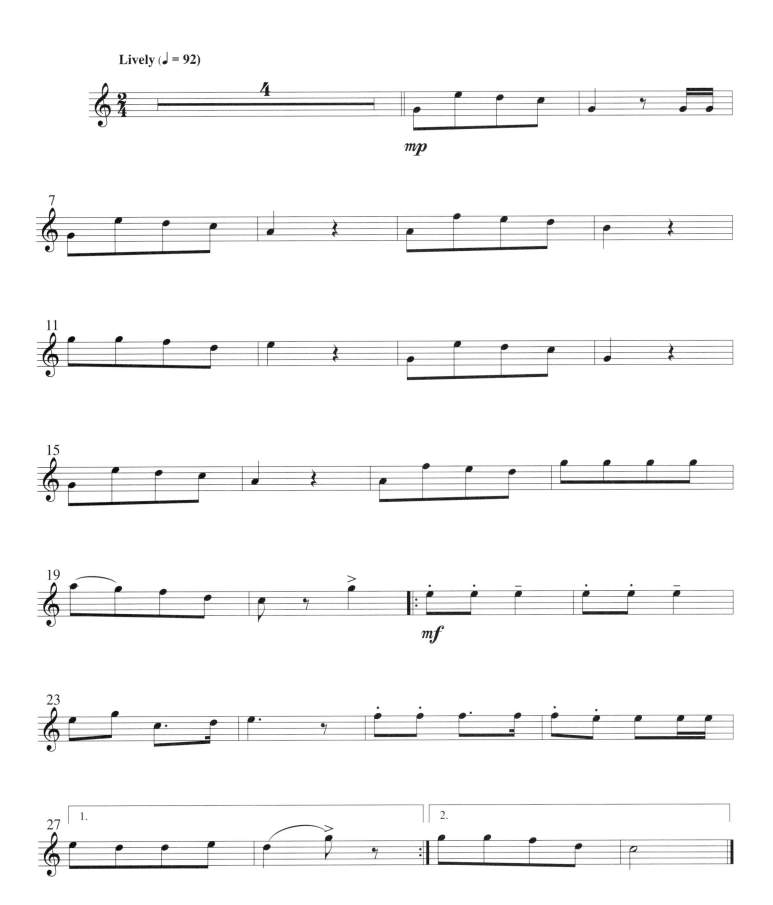

O Come, All Ye Faithful

Adeste Fidelis

Traditional English carol

O, Holy Night

Adolphe Adam (1803–1856)

O Little Town of Bethlehem

Lewis H. Redner (1831–1908)

Moderately flowing (♩ = 84)

The Babe of Bethle'm

Traditional English carol

13

Silent Night

Franz X. Gruber (1787–1863)

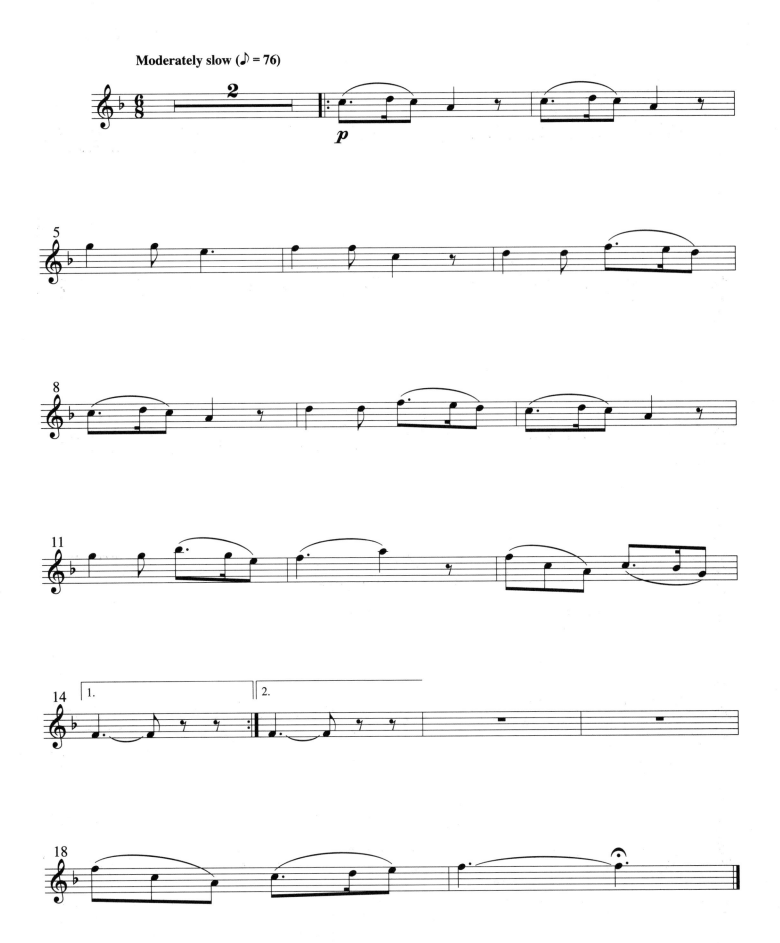

What Child Is This?

Greensleeves

Traditional English air

15

Rocking

Traditional Czech carol

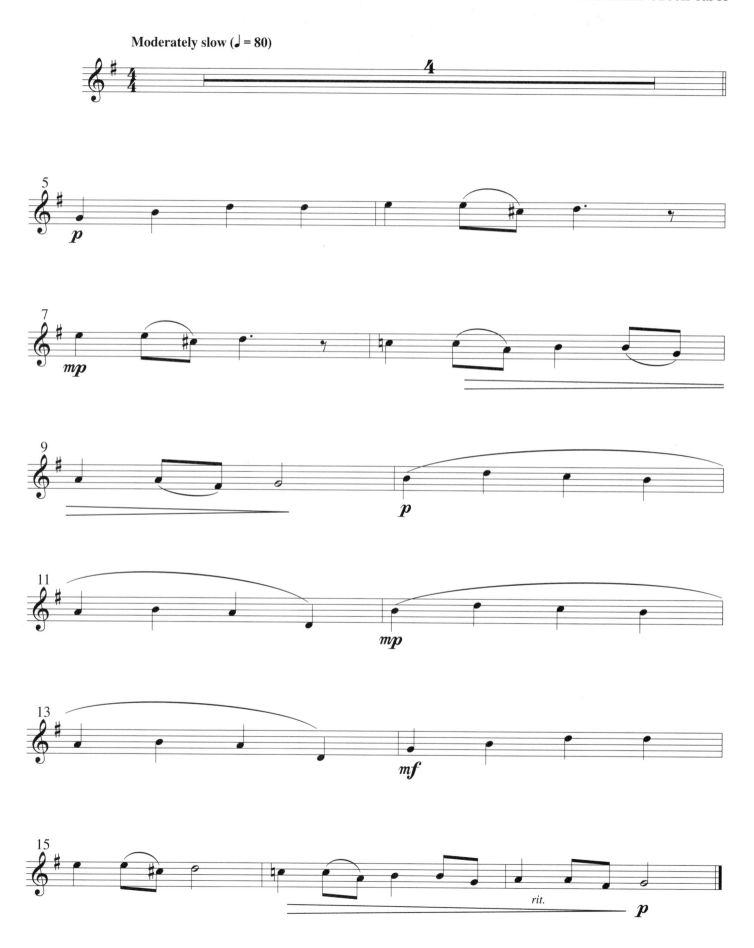

Flute

Angels We Have Heard on High
The Babe of Bethle'm
Deck the Hall
The First Noel
Go, Tell It on the Mountain
God Rest Ye Merry, Gentlemen
I Wonder as I Wander
It Came Upon a Midnight Clear
Jingle Bells
O Come, All Ye Faithful
O, Holy Night
O Little Town of Bethlehem
Rocking
Silent Night
What Child Is This?

O Come, All Ye Faithful

Adeste Fidelis

Traditional English carol

Moderately (♩ = 96)

O, Holy Night

Adolphe Adam (1803–1856)

Slowly (♩. = 60)

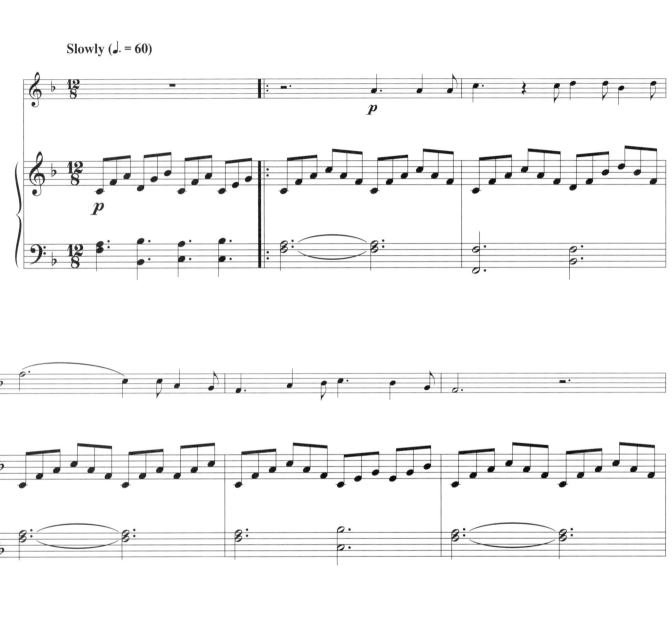

O Little Town of Bethlehem

Lewis H. Redner (1831–1908)

The Babe of Bethle'm

Traditional English carol

Lively (♩ = 132)

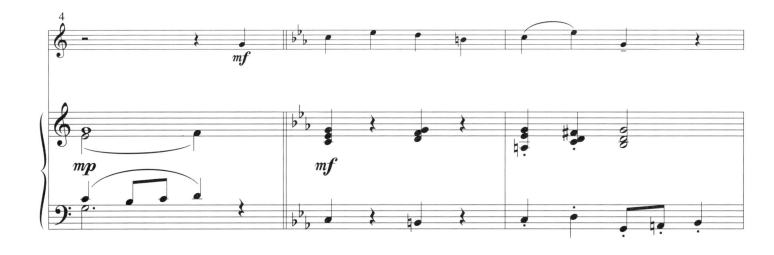

Silent Night

Franz X. Gruber (1787–1863)

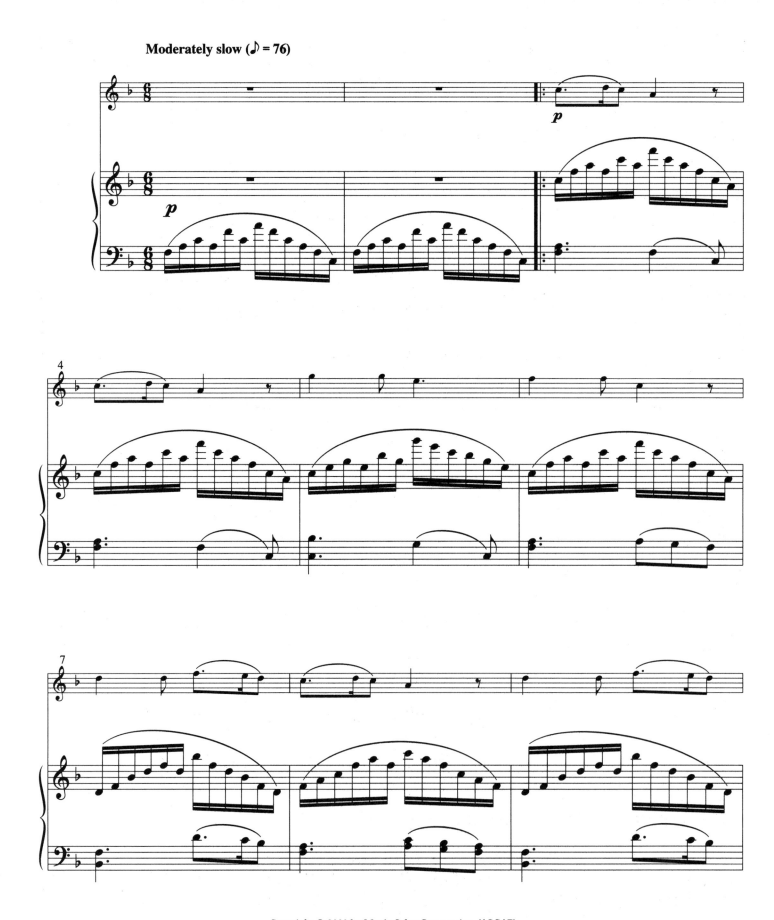

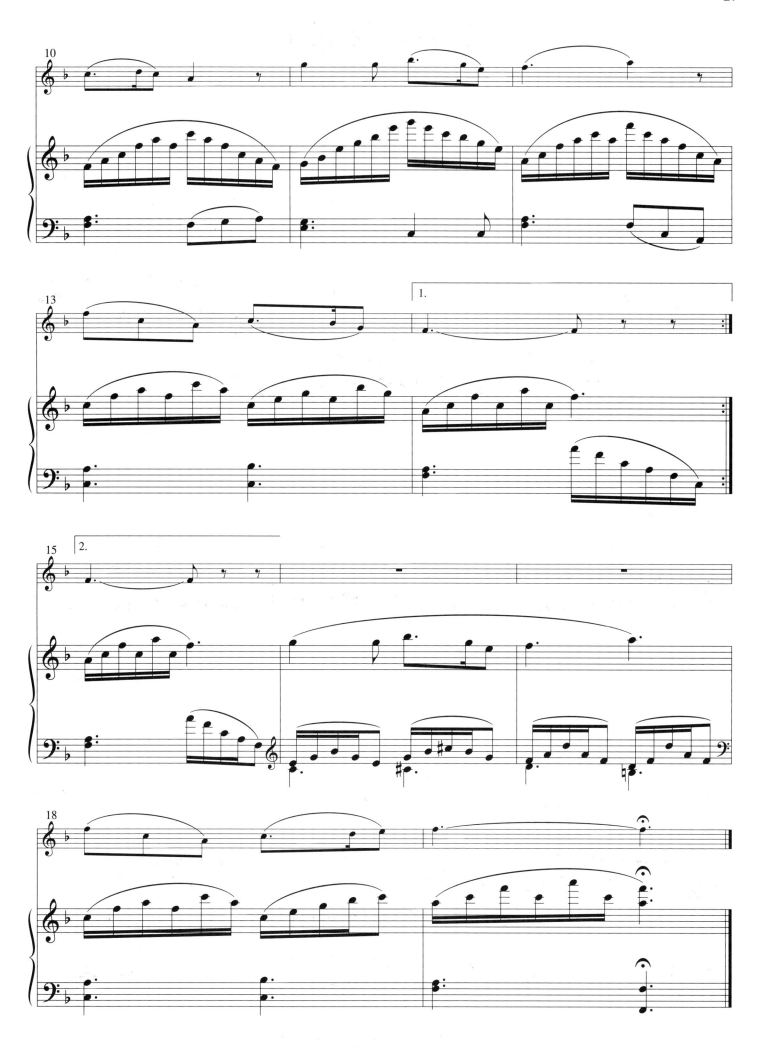

What Child Is This?

Greensleeves

Traditional English air

Moderately (♪ = 126)

Rocking

Traditional Czech carol